RUBANK BOOK OF CLARINET SOLOS
INTERMEDIATE LEVEL

ONLINE MEDIA INCLUDED
Recordings
PDF Accompaniments

CONTENTS

To access recordings and PDF accompaniments visit:
www.halleonard.com/mylibrary

Enter Code
5473-7865-3170-6958

ISBN 978-1-4950-6505-7

RUBANK®

HAL•LEONARD® CORPORATION
7777 W. BLUEMOUND RD. P.O. BOX 13819 MILWAUKEE, WI 53213

Visit Hal Leonard Online at
www.halleonard.com

Adagio And Menuetto

Clarinet

W.A. Mozart
Transcribed by H. Voxman

Clarinet

Fine

TRIO

Menuetto da capo al Fine

4

Alleluja
From "Exsultate, Jubilate"

W. A. Mozart
Edited by H. Voxman

Clarinet

Allegro non troppo

Clarinet

5

Concerto In G Minor

Clarinet

G.F. Handel
Transcribed by H. Voxman

SARABANDE

Largo [♩ = 63]

Clarinet

Chansonette

Clarinet

A.M. Barret
Arranged by A.W. Pazemis

Bel Canto

Clarinet

Clair W. Johnson

Clarinet

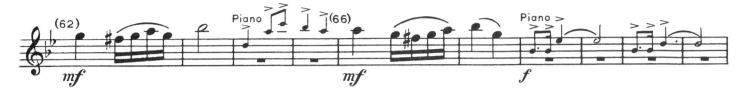

Estilian Caprice

Clarinet

Gene Paul

Fantasy-Piece

Op. 73, No. 1

Clarinet

Robert Schumann
Edited by H. Voxman

Clarinet

Nocturne

From "Concerto in G Minor"

Clarinet

Th. Verhey
Edited by H. Voxman

Clarinet

Tempo I

Lamento

(Nocturne)

Clarinet

L. Bassi
Edited by H. Voxman

Clarinet

Menuet

From "Divertimento in D, K. 334"

Clarinet

W.A. Mozart
Edited by H. Voxman

Clarinet

Romance

Clarinet

Jean Becker
EDITED by H. Voxman